Wandering Spring

Notes from the Woods of Winhall, Vermont

SHIRES ✺ PRESS

4869 Main Street
P.O. Box 2200
Manchester Center, VT 05255
www.northshire.com

Wandering Spring
Notes from the Woods of Winhall, Vermont

ISBN Number: 978-1-60571-326-7

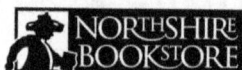

NORTHSHIRE BOOKSTORE

Building Community, One Book at a Time
*A family-owned, independent bookstore in
Manchester Ctr., VT, since 1976 and Saratoga Springs, NY since 2013.
We are committed to excellence in bookselling.
The Northshire Bookstore's mission is to serve as a resource for
information, ideas, and entertainment while honoring the needs of
customers, staff, and community.*

Printed in the United States of America

Wandering

Spring

Notes from the Woods
of Winhall, Vermont

J. E. Diaz

For Suzie

Inspiration, Sounding Board, Grounding Rod.

Thank You

Preface

I can hear my grandmother Ida in a searing, accented voice, tight-fingered flat hand beside her head waving at forty forty-five degrees yelling, "Vagabondo! Cafone! Get a job!" An early 20th century immigrant, Grandma had no patience for any activity that wasn't centered on work or earning money. "You gotta be somebody," was her favorite admonition. For her, wandering the woods was akin to wasting your time and wasting your mind. For others it's a romantic notion filled with innocent ideas of strolling bucolic byways, or perhaps an idealistic dream, free of the demands of everyday life. For me, it's work (Grandma would be proud, though the lack of income wouldn't impress her). But in the interest of not losing your trust, I have to admit it's a labor of love. "Do what you love," was another of Grandma Ida's admonitions, though this one she'd whisper to me quietly when no one else was around. She knew by the wonder in my eyes when she told stories of *her* grandfather wandering the Alps that *his* blood courses *my* veins.

So, as a young lad in my late teens I set off with a backpack and a plan; approach Bear Mountain in lower New York State from the south on the Appalachian Trial, climb the mountain, then head north for eleven days. Wherever I ended up, I'd find a phone booth (what's that?) and call home for a pick up. I never made it.

Once I spied the surrounding landscape from the summit of Bear Mountain, I lost all aspirations of being a distance hiker and decided to wander Bear Mountain and Harriman State Park. When I began exploring the Catskills it was the same thing; wander certain areas instead of hiking through them. My graduation to the Green Mountains in Vermont followed like pattern as Stratton, Winhall, and Manchester became my new haunt. A short time in the Whites of New Hampshire added new experiences in the east, but a stint in the mountains and deserts of Utah for a month long survival experience put a pause in my eastern wandering until finally moving to the area in '83. Lye Brook Wilderness beckoned and then the Grout Pond/Somerset area drew my attention. More time in Utah's mountains, some in Arizona, some more in the Sierra Nevada of California, a bit in Colorado, Montana and Wyoming, Alberta, British Columbia, the Smokey Mountains of North Carolina, Gaspe Quebec, Switzerland, Italy, Colombia, Argentina, and Chile, as well as wandering the woods here at home, all compel me to make the following statement: Winhall is as beautiful a place as any other place such as this.

Contents

Introduction:

Invitation

Life is a journey of discovery. But not all discoveries are firsts and that's ok. Nature designed it that way so we could all experience what discovery feels like. Have you ever seen the face of a child learning to walk?

Like those steps, one after another, every piece in this book consists of, was inspired by, is a result of, or otherwise recollects a journey not only into the woods, but a journey that led to another journey and so on and so on. As with any journey, there's usually some sort of idea of how you'd like things to turn out i.e. on survival we all wanted to survive. But preconceived ideas often get in the way of learning and personally, I'd rather be led on a journey of discovery than have the answer handed to me.

The most important component built into the survival experience in Utah had to be "discovered." No one held our hand. We had to find our way and survive along it. We learned that survival is a readied state of mind, free of the encumbrances of preconception. And while this Is not a book on survival, nor am I suggesting the reader take a month out of their life and stumble around the woods, I am challenging you to experience the ancient learning process of discovery, hence the books sparse reference to specific locations and the sometimes elusive allusions to timeframe.

In addition, I get tired of stories ending neat and tidy following a predictable pattern to an anticipated end. That's not real. Unanswered questions, open-ended conclusions, interesting and boring stuff, as well as things you remember and things you'd rather forget all happen in a given day in the woods. The structure of many of the stories reflects this reality.

Now, let's go wandering. But be warned. There is a great danger lurking in the woods that sets wandering apart from other outdoor experiences. Wandering comes with the inherent risk of having no schedule to follow and no particular place to be.

Bearings

Long before the first Native peoples wandered into an area that the British would later incorporate into what is now our town, nature designed Winhall with snow and ice; accumulating for tens of thousands of years, glaciers sculpted the land before melting away leaving two Sentinels that have been watching over this area ever since. Bromley Mountain with its legendary south facing ski slopes and Stratton Mountain with its well known north facing slopes mark the north and south boundaries of the town. The Appalachian/Long Trail meanders in the west while Gale Meadows Pond is the prominent landmark in the east.

The location of Winhall relative to the Great Lakes, Lake Champlain, the Hudson River basin, the Adirondacks, the White Mountains, the Connecticut River basin, the Atlantic Ocean, the northern tip of the Taconic Range, and the local Green Mountains and their watersheds, has a profound effect on the weather, changing it often.

Pagan Sacred

My eyes struggle to follow a faint trail of disturbed leaves through the dormant, snowless woods, while the moon; cold, bright, white in the southwest, illuminates my way. Familiar celestial bodies guide me: Sirius is setting in the west, high in the sky is Jupiter to the south, and the Big Dipper is overhead; its outer edge ever faithful in pointing north to Polaris. I continue walking, reading leaf litter and sky and noting the shadow creatures that watch me. For as many times as I've done this you'd think the shadow creatures wouldn't surprise me anymore. But they do, every time. Resisting the urge to disperse them with the aid of a headlamp, I arrive at my destination by moonlight, thirty minutes before Vernal Equinox.

Earlier in the week I gathered wood and re-set a few stones at this old fire pit in anticipation of honoring the pagan sacred; welcoming the change of season by firelight. Though it seems sacrilegious at this moment to defile the holy, moon-lit darkness with man-made fire, I embrace the ancient ritual, appeasing the spirits of my ancestors.

Warm and inviting on this first moment of spring the colors of sunrise flicker in the light of my hardwood fire, and in the wee-est hour of the morning, at 00:31, Vernal Equinox arrives. Crossing the equator on its journey north, the sun promises once again that life will flourish in our hemisphere.

Within an hour my last winter-lit fire passes quietly into the night and the woods return to celestial light. I drift off, no longer an anomaly in the forest, but part of it.

First Day on Earth

My eyes open to the dim glow of dawn. As though it were my first day on earth, I'm in awe of the scene before me. Grey-orange horizon with pale blue above yields to a twilight sky overhead, while night still rules the west. Light filters in; shadows become trees and open spaces; shadow. Brown-red replaces grey-orange in the east and rocks, sticks, and leaves begin to take shape, form, and color in the surrounding sepia light. The air is still. A small seasonal stream trickles nearby. Sitting on the ground absorbing the energy of the moment; of life in the Universe, of what it is to be alive, I'm in the fabled Tír na nÓg here in the woods of Winhall as last winter night turns to first spring day.

Sunrise… 12°F. I shiver and quake in the cold morning air. Hypothermia has a foothold… time to move.

Big Rock

There's a particular big rock along one of the many log roads in Winhall that has apparently moved from one side of the road to the other. It's a curious thing to see such a large object out of place though how it moved is not mysterious given its proximity to the road. Upside down from its former orientation, this chalk-grey chunk of glacial till seems content in its new position; well situated and angled so as to offer a comfortable seat. I accept the invitation.

Looking at what happened here it's easy to imagine being stuck in one's station in life year after year as all else around flourishes; being buried alive by the debris of other's lives isn't uncommon. But *this rock*, having been dislodged from its former confinement has a new outlook, and the muck-filled depression on the other side of the road is proof enough that Nature dislikes voids and wastes no time in filling them. Life it would seem is fluid, and staying stuck in one place is, well, for rocks.

As it turns out, this big rock is the finest of companions. It supports me unconditionally and never disagrees. Likewise I often thank it for being who it is and never say anything bad about it. I can tell it anything that happens to be on my mind and it listens without ever showing the slightest hint of being bored, shocked, or disappointed by anything said. Big Rock and I have become friends and I'm a better man because of it.

Small Glacial Moraine

One of my favorite places along the Mill Brook is where there appears to be the remnant of a small glacial moraine covered with evergreens. It's an anonymous place with good cover. The ridgeline of this feature is used by the local coyote clan and there's often fresh scat somewhere along its length. Getting there is always fun no matter which route I pick.

. . .

Today I find myself slipping on ice formed from a previous overflow of the brook. The March sun can't penetrate dense, overhanging hemlocks here, so ice persists on an otherwise snowless forest floor along the brook, despite recent warm weather. Blocks of ice deposited by storm swell litter the water's edge. It's difficult to imagine this stream heaving car size pieces of ice up and out of its waters.

At my destination I climb the slender hill's north end while an easterly breeze, heavy with the scent of hemlock, cools me. Soft forest duff muffles my approach; the roaring brook dampens it. Pretending to travel with stealth, I continue the game; any variation in my behavior likely to trigger the flight impulse in whatever may be watching.

The wind shifts; out of the north now, no chance of sneaking up on anything in front of me on the ridge.

Assuming disclosure with the shifting wind, my pace quickens to the top of the feature where I'm scolded by two ravens leaping into the air, scrambling for a perch and their dignity. It's obvious I startled them and they're not going to let me forget it. I happen to like ravens so I sit down and begin talking to them. Ravens listen well, but only if they're interested in what you have to say. I apologize for spooking them, explaining it was not my intent as I had given up the game of sneaking once the wind was at my back. Unable to save face after being so startled they take flight, croaking and complaining to each other at how rude I was. At least that's what it sounds like to me.

Well, no matter, the woods are quiet again except for the roar of the brook.

Knock Wood

For the most part our mammalian kin who live in the Northeast are a mild mannered bunch. Every now and then though, for whatever reason, they become intolerant of our intrusions.

Mistakes happen when wandering in the woods; we come upon things like dens, nests, and burrows, we get in between mothers and their babies, we disturb the euphoric pining of love-crazed bull moose etc. Sometimes our safety depends on our reaction. Though panicking is inappropriate, backing away from a surprised and stressed animal standing its ground is proper etiquette and may defuse an unpleasant encounter. I'd rather walk away from an animal that has a reason to stand its ground than challenge it in its home. Though in the case of bees, wasps, and hornets, panic *is* appropriate and running, *preferred*.

So far (knocking the wooden table I'm writing from) the above approach has worked for me in situations which have included moose, bear, coyote, bobcat, fisher, raccoon, woodchuck, beaver, a very angry goose, a psychotic territorial Red squirrel, an adorable yet ferocious Little Brown bat, and yes, even an immeasurable multitude of maniacal wasps (you thought I was kidding about the wasps?). Whether or not any of these animals carried rabies at the time, I do not know, but I have yet to witness clinical signs of rabies in any animals I've crossed paths with (knocking wood again).

So what will be your approach when wandering in the woods should you come across one of our mammalian kin with young, or near their den, or near a cache, or in some stage of courtship ritual? Will you stand your ground, or walk away out of respect? Will you be honest with yourself and accept the fact that you're not welcome, or provoke an otherwise docile creature because you think you have a right to be in that spot? Will you act out of fear; thinking all animals attack, or out of arrogance; thinking no animal will ever attack you?

Marking My Territory

Norway Spruces are majestic trees when grown in the open with room to spread their limbs. They're so common in our woods that many people don't realize they're a non-indigenous species. As the name would imply, they're hardy trees; well suited to the environs of Vermont, though my understanding is that they originated somewhere in Eastern Europe. There's a particular grove of these beauties along one of the wonderfully open log roads in Winhall. Beyond the Norway spruce grove the trail leads to an open area recently logged, with rejected material strewn about, and large piles of brush pushed along the woods edge. It's a jumble of a habitat.

As is my custom, I shy away from walking out into open spaces when wandering in the woods. I circumnavigate the area to stay within cover, but I have to pee and that's all I can think of. While taking a moment to relieve myself near a large brush pile that's been shoved into the woods edge, the bark of a Red squirrel seems just another inconsequential and rather un-noteworthy sound in the forest. But that sound grows very non-*Tamiasciurus* and I sense that something is quite squirrely indeed. Before I can finish the business at hand, my ears hasten to tell my brain (which is not firing rapidly at the moment) that it should cease and desist and begin locomotion whether or not the currently engaged appendage is securely fastened for departure.

Because of my carelessness, I've been perceived marking as *my territory*, the entrance to a bobcat den which may or may not contain kittens. But what matters most right now is that at least one occupant is mad, and rightly so. "What an idiot," I think to myself while walking the straightest line away from the growling and hissing brush pile, taking me out into the open. I feel naked... and stupid. It's difficult to walk on such uneven, log-strewn ground while one eye is watching behind and the other is navigating forward direction through the jumble. Falling is not in my best interest right now.

About 50 feet away the vehement growling continues but the overall objection is devoid of hissing. I take that as a good sign and keep walking; each step I take away from my mistake soothes my injured pride. I have to remind myself that all of us who've spent time in the woods trying to go unnoticed have betrayed our presence through carelessness. Something as simple as a bio-function impulse (though to be fair mine was quite urgent), and we forget where we are. I acted like a troll and was rightly perceived as such.

Finally at about 200 yards... quiet.

Getting back into cover I position myself with a good line of sight to the brush pile. Scanning every inch of it with binoculars I struggle to make a cat out of sticks and branches, but not even my vivid imagination can create such things from the light entering my objective lenses.

Twenty minutes... forty minutes... an hour. I resist the urge to head back. It's getting late in the day and I have no headlamp or flashlight with me. An hour and twenty... an hour and forty... Wait... what is that? Obscured by twigs and sticks a grayish form appears at the brush pile as an apparition. It's not moving. I try to breathe quietly as the excitement quickens my respiration, and at once it disappears.

And that's all I saw.

.

Chicken Sandwich

A post-equinox sun warms my clothes through the dormant canopy, cold north winds bite into them. Treetops high-five each other as the wind conducts a clacking symphony above me. Below the sway, shadows dance on snow-dusted ground. The Winhall River roaring behind me, I wander north along one of the many small streams flowing into it. The usual mix of merry minstrels bids me good day; I enjoy the chorus of titmice, chickadees, and nuthatches as we travel together.

My companions continue on, more interested in their business than mine. I must seem silly to them, traveling without the slightest interest in foraging and not appearing the least bit concerned for my safety. But maybe that's why they traveled with me for as long as they did. Safety in numbers is one thing, traveling with a friendly giant is something else altogether. For who dares to challenge a giant with such carefree confidence?

Chuckling, I clear a small ridge and notice movement along the stream below me. Raising my binoculars, I focus on the movement; nothing appears. Then it materializes; a coyote stares at me from the other side of the rivulet. It seems unafraid. We continue walking upstream; the coyote on its side, I on mine, happy to have noticed the movement and see something in my binoculars.

The ravine is a precarious place for birds aloft; tomahawks of turbulence hack into the hillside as cold north winds clash with rising thermals above this south facing slope. I look forward to finding a wind sheltered spot to nap later. Stopping for a sip of water, another movement catches my eye and I spy the coyote again. This time it's off to my east, a little further away than last. Thirst quenched, I continue.

Far above the river, the sound of it muffled, wind more than makes up for the absence of its roar, so much so that I haven't realized until now how high above it I am. I search for a good place to nap. The coyote again presents itself, now half the distance away than before. More hungry than alarmed, I sit on the ground, reach into my pack and pull out a chicken sandwich loosely wrapped in a cloth napkin. "Of course," I think to myself, sighing. "Why don't you just drag some carrion behind you for good measure?"

Instinct rules the moment springing me upward as my new friend trots toward me. It stops when I reach my feet and looks around. I follow its gaze... One coyote... Two coyote... Three coyote... Finding a nearby rock to sit on, I begin talking in a loud enough voice for them all to hear, laughing as I speak.

"While *I am* willing to share *my* lunch, *I am not* willing to be *your* lunch."

No reply.

. . .

I finished the sandwich that day and continued to search for a good place to nap... never did find it. Though a bit startled at being approached and seeing three together, I know coyotes to be opportunists and they smelled opportunity in the form of a loosely wrapped chicken sandwich, not me. Once I finished it, the opportunity had passed... I didn't see them the rest of the day.

And that's all that happened.

One Thing I Do Well

Low and faint in a post dawn sky, the flexed bow of a waning crescent moon takes aim at the horizon. The path of its would-be arrow betrays the place where the sun will rise. Before I can loose another imaginary shot, a point of orange light heralds the rising sun which wastes no time clearing distant mountains, casting its now yellow light across a snow-covered landscape. My eyes are blinded by the combined brightness of its direct and reflected light. Spots of grey haunt my vision as I look away, blinking.

Sixteen days after bidding farewell to winter it's 8°F. A coyote, Red -breasted nuthatch, and Blue jay break the morning silence. A west wind gusts. Swirling snow from nearby spruces envelopes me in a scene from a snow globe, chilling my face and stinging my nose. Five inches of new snow underfoot adds to the deception and for a moment it's late January or early February. Though not terribly uncommon for April 6th, the temperature is unwelcome, at least by me, but the snow, the glorious snow... I'm out early to see what's moving around and where it's going. Besides, in snow I'm less likely to get lost, which is one thing I do well.

Following a set of coyote tracks, I wander into an open area. There's a single goldenrod plant, broken half way from its top with the dry remnant of its flower cluster hanging, drawing a 120° arc in the snow centered exactly south of the stem; its motion fueled by a steady north wind.

Pendulum-like in movement, it has the precision of a Swiss watch; 60° west, 60° east etc. etc. "What an odd thing to notice," I think to myself. Continuing my "pursuit" of the coyote I begin to notice something that has far more reaching implications than a goldenrod timepiece.

For an hour I've followed the tracks of this animal down an old log road. Along the way, it avoided every low wet spot, every thin-ice covered water pocket, every muck-filled depression covered in snow. This coyote wished to keep its paws as dry as possible; a deliberate and conscious act of forethought; a sign of higher intelligence. So by what standard do we judge the intelligence, or even creativity of these animals?

And speaking of creativity, does this explain the reason otters slide along snow covered terrain wherever and whenever possible? Spotting the tell tale trough near where I had stopped to ponder the coyote question, I change direction and follow the meandering trail of an otter. Traveling over and under downed trees and limbs, this wonderful animal seems to have melted over everything instead of using quadrupedal motion. Following a wide, former stream bed it made its way into what seems for me, an impenetrable spruce thicket. Crawling for while, I follow the tracks along the snowless, soft duff.

"It's thick in here," I think to myself. "Where am I?" is my next thought.

"Great."

Another Thing I Do Well

Unable to convince myself to go back through the spruce thicket the way I came, I continue reading otter tracks and crawling along the dampening duff. With each limb placement, I notice the ground getting wetter. There's an open area ahead. "Of course it's open. It's a swamp," I think to myself as I stand up, surrounded and supported by countless saplings of spruce and fir. The smell of Christmas fills my nose while the gauntlet of branches pokes, pierces, and pushes against every step. Eyes squinted, blinking quick and slight, with arms crossed in front of my face, I break through the wall.

"This is a problem," I mutter, my words echoing in the solitude of this swampy bowl. On the edge of an almost perfect circle, enclosed by spruce/fir thicket, I stand an unsuspecting prisoner who stumbled into his cell. The spooky sounds of a windblown spruce grove echo in every direction; whining, creaking, moaning, and haunting meows like those of kittens lend eeriness to the scene. It's painfully cold in the shade. I close my eyes and quiet my thoughts.

. . .

Thoughts stilled, my eyes open. This ethereal corral, the beauty and solitude, now reminds me of the reason I wander. No experience can replace this one. No other place is this place. No other time is this time. There is no problem now than the one that exists in the fact that I cannot stay here forever. How healing is the forest that it can change our outlook in minutes. What energy is there out here that permeates our being? Is it that of trees? Does it take a forest full of them to have this effect?

The "Granola Bar" session over, I feel lighter than I did when I arrived. Snow blowing from distant trees dissipates toward the forest floor in a reverse performance of summer mists disappearing up and out of the canopy. A flock of Pine siskin descends on the swamp. The sight and sound is overwhelming. Revived, I head back.

. . .

After a double-check of the map and compass, I got myself pointed in the right direction that day; crawling, stumbling, and walking to get un-lost. It's another thing I do well.

Ethereal Echoes

Cornflake leaves on the dry ground of dormant woods announce my approach to the beaver pond. Even earthworms make noise in this stuff. I give up on the idea of secrecy, hurry to a small flat spot and set up my tiny screen tent in seconds. In the fading light of day, Jupiter and the Moon reflect in the still water until ripples from the resident beaver's disapproving tail slap stretch and bend their reflected light.

Stoking a deep-bowled churchwarden I settle in for the evening performance already in progress. Wood frogs perform, "We're really little ducks" in ensemble. Spring peepers feign tepidity, beginning with an aria before committing themselves to a full peeping chorale. Percussive sapsuckers tap their staccato interlude from across the pond as sunset draws the curtain on scene one.

Beginning scene two, "Etude for Hermit Thrush" evokes all that is good in me. Exquisite flutist unequaled, a Hermit kindles the romantic flame of soul and awakens beauty in the beast. Barbarian and Refined are equally moved for none can resist the enchantment of its voice. Its ethereal echoes play their fugue until, without pause or warning; earthly silence... except for the frogs that carry on like unruly children at recital.

Whiffs of fresh water pond; clean, yet of mud, waft through the tent as I slip into the nylon cocoon of my sleeping bag. The finale begins as the resident gander blows his warning horn from weedy shallows. His mate lies motionless in the moonlight atop her nest on the beaver lodge. A pair of Barred owls call, one deep in the woods, the other at water's edge. Good reason for alarm. This scene will play multiple times while goose eggs hatch and goslings waddle. Peepers and Wood frogs inspired by darkness whip into a frenzied antithesis of unison; an atonal encore despite audience indifference.

Many footsteps stir the night, though even by the bright light of a waxing moon I see nothing but shadow creatures.

I drift off...

The thumping of a Ruffed grouse stirs me. The moon is low in the west. Peepers quiet, Wood frogs lessen.

I drift off again....

Owls announce the setting moon. I measure time by the movement of space as stars cross the sky in their unfailing pageantry.

At peace with the Universe, I sleep soundly.

. . .

A Hermit thrush heralds a new day at dawn. Only the sweet whisper of a lover's voice can match its beauty. There's another Hermit to the east; deeper voiced, and a third on the north hill; more exquisite than the others, its voice; melodious melancholy.

Dawn brightens. Blaring caterwaul fills the hollow as Barred owls announce their presence. The gander stays silent, the goose, still. Two deer stare at my tent, tails flicking. A tom turkey performs his fan tailed rendition of "I'm a Bad-Ass Rooster" for his harem. The grouse continues "Thumping for Lovers" where it left off before moonset as Wood frogs begin singing "We're really little ducks" again. Sapsuckers perform "Squeak and Bob" while robins play "Peep and Fight." Hairy and Downy woodpeckers busy themselves with breakfast. A phoebe seems lost; bobbing its tail, repeating its name, while the Hermit on the north hill continues its gentle etude of pleasing sadness.

And I lay still, quiet; unwilling to disturb their world with zip of plastic and swish of nylon.

The Highlands

The Highlands are a lovely, lonely area in April. Each season has its beauty here, but navigating the deciduous woods is easier in early spring. Once the weather warms and leaves open, much of it becomes a dense forest fortress guarded by legions of black flies, mosquitoes, deer flies, and ticks, where blood and sweat are the price of passage and unpreparedness can drive you mad. Though it is beautiful in the warmer months despite these annoyances, that beauty passes quickly. It's a short growing season up here lasting barely three months between leaf out and the onset of autumn.

. . .

Today there's a dusting of snow; a white backdrop in every direction. Cloudy skies with strong west winds intensify the 27°F air temperature. It's cold. A pair of Mallards, indifferent to my presence, watches me skirt the edge of their half-frozen little pond. The swamps are devoid of life except for what stirs at their edges and bottoms, unseen.

Even with a winter such as the one that just passed, with a deplorable lack of snow, the numerous streams here in the south Highlands run full and loud draining both east into the Winhall, and west into the Battenkill.

The inherent beauty of a Highlands spring lies in its weather; dry, cold and windy one day, warmer, humid and still, the next. Snow can and does fall through May, yet the day after a dusting, black flies can bite with ferocity. Any day can be cold and dry, then snow, turn warm and humid, rain a bit and be buggy all in the same day.

This doesn't seem to bother the creatures that live up here as evidenced by the amount of scat visible today. I imagine the mild winter has seen an increase in the numbers of animals that stayed high this year.

There are endless places for dens and to hole up. Garage-sized boulders in varying stages of decay surrounded and topped by trees and tree roots, forest debris, and seasonal plants strewn about, create more than enough nooks and crannies to harbor many of our mammalian kin that call this place home.

In The Shade of

Spruce, Fir and Hemlock

West winds mask my approach as I arrive at the southern end of the beaver pond undetected by Hooded mergansers in the north. Ice clings to shadow at the foot of the dam. Layers of mud, stick and rock blur the line between order and chaos; cognitive art expressed in a structure built by rodents. And it's strong.

Six feet high by twelve feet long, this wall is holding back nineteen-hundred tons of water as the pond measures over two-hundred feet by one-hundred twenty feet with an average depth of two and a half feet. Without engineering degrees, machinery, or internet access for ideas, a family of beaver did this. So by what standard do we judge the intelligence or creativity of these creatures?

As seeps surround my feet I ponder the consequence of collapse before sneaking up to get a frog's eye view of the water. Only my eyes and top of my head rise above its surface. A beaver swims zigzag across the pond in a slow approach to the dam. Nostrils widen and narrow in rhythm with its stroke. Calm eyes convey the peace of the moment.

At twenty feet away my presence is noticed. Blinking eyes and flared nostrils denote a change in emotion as the beaver swims toward me, head rising out of the water like the bow of a boat as it accelerates. I've appeared too suddenly, too close. I stay put. It's not time for sudden movement. Before reaching the wall, Old Saw Tooth makes a sharp turn and submerges with a slap of the tail sending simultaneous concussive and liquid waves in an outward expanding circle. I chuckle as the splash radius reaches me.

Slinking away, I follow the seep to the next pond and examine the dam there. Not nearly as glorious as the upper pond's dam, this one holds back enough water for the beavers to dig canals for travel, but the average water level hasn't changed for two decades. After a thorough examination of the wall, I slip into the evergreens on the west shore.

Staying in the shade of spruce, fir and hemlock is a cold proposition today, but worth the exchange of cover it provides. While listening to Spring peepers play hide and go peep and the varying conversations of Wood frogs from pond to pond, I see something moving in the hardwoods at the south end. A look through binoculars reveals a woodcock, probing leaf litter at every step.

Cold air sifts through my clothes, chilling my skin. Still I wait, watching from the cover of my shady blind. Leaves rustle behind me; footsteps, lithe and swift trot toward me, then stop. I've been found. A question of etiquette comes to mind; what's the polite thing to do now?

Fighting the urge to turn, I stay motionless. A slight breeze from behind yields no clue of scent. Slow, methodic breathing, though not deep, keeps my heart rate manageable as I deny primitive instincts to turn and see what's there. My thoughts wander. I've been in this situation before. Each time it ended with the animal walking or running away, sometimes vocalizing its distain, sometimes not. What will happen today?

A piercing bark spins my head around. A Red fox bolts through the forest like a Hollywood Superhero.

Startled and smiling I stand up to leave.

Shivers assail me.

I'm hypothermic.

It's difficult to walk.

Along The River

The cerulean sky is a stunning sight. A blazing sun blinds me. Crisp wind sans odor purges my lungs; the rush of it deafens my ears. Cool air upstream, cold water down, in the river bed I ponder the current juxtaposition. A Red-tailed hawk shadows me from above. I make the mistake of looking for it, glancing back into the sun. A faint, descending shriek gives hint at its presence now beyond the edge of the ravine.

Along the river, boulders, trees, limbs, gravel bars, sandbars, islands and pools create varied habitat and a puzzle to navigate. I avoid the post-Irene debris piles that catch a foot and twist a leg. There are numerous slides along the river; reminders that erosion is a process that has no end.

Near the confluence of the river and one of its more reliable tributaries, an island in the widened streambed suggests an earlier, greater event than Hurricane Irene. The banks of the stream there are steep and rise above the island. A gap in the southern bank hints at the rising water's escape route from a debris-clogged confluence.

The first wave of migratory songbirds has already returned to their birthplaces in the forest as spring approaches its second trimester. Hermit thrushes and phoebes have arrived from points south and Song sparrows and kingfishers from lower elevations. A few of the hardier resident robins wintered along the Winhall, but more are arriving, mixing with the locals, adding their melodies (and soon their genes) to the year round residents'. Chickadees, nuthatches, Brown creepers, Blue jays and titmice are also present, as is the tiny and tenacious Golden-crowned kinglet. This bird is a lesson in humility. What it can endure is beyond any of us.

Crowded communities of tiny yellow violets and low growing grasses stretch beyond their daily production of chlorophyll, the warming soil beneath pushing them into competition for precious space. Fresh Partridgeberry leaves feel and smell rubbery, reminiscent of birthday balloons. Trout lily's mottled leaves unfurl in the late morning sun, Dutchman's Breeches' lacy dark green foliage contrasts the broad, green-leaved trillium soon to flower, while Spring Beauties already in bloom spread along the leaf litter in a sparse, incontinuous carpet. Bumble bees brave the still chill winds to drink the nectar of these tiny white and pink flowers as thrust from their wings lay down the soft, flimsy plants.

Many trails cross the one I'm on but deer tracks dominate the imprint inventory. They too are migrating, following the line of green growth and swelling buds and twigs as it moves up the ravine into the surrounding forest. Less dramatic than Mule deer migrations of the West, our Whitetails nonetheless move with the food and cover availability throughout the year.

Earth Day

...Fascinating concept; Earth Day. I don't think the Earth knows it's Earth Day, and maybe that's a good thing. Perhaps she would celebrate her special day with the dancing of tectonic plates, or the fireworks of an eruption at Yellowstone. We wouldn't think that was a very nice Earth Day now would we. Why one day; Earth Day, when everything we need or want comes from the Earth every day?

To my knowledge all the world's great religions honor god at least once a week, and he's been an absentee father for millennium while the Earth suffers a mother's fate; underappreciated, recognized but once a year. I say, let's start giving Mom a place of honor in our weekly gatherings and let her know we love her.

. . .

It's a mild morning. The air is still. There's a flurry of activity as woodpeckers and kin dominate the woodland conversation.

In the distance, Yellow-bellied sapsuckers propose their borders with short, quick rolling taps lengthened by slowing tempo and rests in notation. A Downy's rapid, repetitive staccato from a resonant tree makes a far bigger impression of it than what its size conveys. Like a small child discovering for the first time it can make noise, mesmerized by its own achievement, not wholly aware of what it's doing, it continues the petition for territory. The maniacal laugh of a Pileated gives the illusion of preceding it up the hillside. Two Hairy's answer each other with bursts of tiny jackhammer, furious in their race to establish which one will win their land claim. The Pileated's choice of hollowed tree affirms *its* border as log-drum-echoes cross the valley. A Northern flicker joins the fray and if I didn't see it through my binoculars I'd assume it was another Hairy hammering, as their three-pitched ensemble lilts through the dormant wood. A newcomer to the neighborhood, a Red-bellied, late to the gathering, nonetheless bids on a property with its rendition of repetitious staccato not unlike the Downy's. With all the bustle of a woodland construction project with a deadline, these percussive creatures are the only audible birds right here, right now.

As I ponder what a unique moment in time this is, a childlike grin spreads across my face. I feel like a kid who's been given a present for the occasion. I can even hear Mom singing, "...Happy Earth Day to You."

The Highlands II

About one third of a month later...

The 34°F on my thermometer feels much warmer due to sunny skies, calm winds, and the perceived warmth of a snowless landscape. As I travel along the Wilderness border a robin walks and flits in front of me as though it were my guide or scout, staying just far enough away to alert me of any "danger." It seems bent on getting me to go faster, so I entertain the fantastical notion and quicken my pace. After several minutes of this hurriedness, my guide veers off into the woods in an uncharacteristically quiet airborne escape while at that moment a fisher crosses in front of me in the same line of sight as the exiting robin, not ten yards away. I stop. A Ruffed grouse springs from the ground onto a low branch out of the immediate reach of the fisher. The cat seems disinterested and focused on something else as it continues on its course and pace. Looking through binoculars I hope to bring it in closer... It's gone.

I like fishers. I've seen quite a number of them over the years both at my house and while wandering. What I don't like is when they select one of my cats as a menu item. Still, I've never thought of destroying one. On the contrary, if you've ever seen or have the opportunity to see one, consider yourself fortunate. You're in a limited group. To see these miniature wolverines at work is a marvel you won't soon forget.

The amount and variety of scat has increased since I was here earlier in the month. I'm not a scatologist, but there are several "varieties" and multiple examples of each. Bear and coyote are clearly represented as is most likely Red fox and raccoon. And judging by the similarity to what I find in the litter box at home, I'll make the assumption that Bobcat is also represented. As for the rest, my limited skills in this craft yield to the term "inconclusive." One thing that *is* obvious is the lack of moose droppings. Twenty years ago it seemed every day in the Highlands was a day you'd see moose or evidence thereof. Today (meaning literally this day) there's no sign of their scat, fresh or otherwise. My understanding is that the winter tick population explosion and the Whitetail's brain worm is taking a toll on moose here as in other states.

What appears to be a broken turkey egg catches my attention as I walk by it. It sizes up as turkey; tan color with various sized brownish speckles, but it's early for turkey eggs. The timing seems more reasonable for woodcock at lower elevation… another item for the "inconclusive" list. As much as I enjoy solving mysteries out here, I also enjoy not being able to answer every question. If I knew it all, what fun would it be?

I contemplate this as I walk into a small cloud of mayflies and notice a pair of Hermit thrushes flitting about and searching for food, exploring the forest floor. Hermits are rugged birds, arriving earlier and leaving later than most people realize. The first one I saw this year was a male over a week ago early in the morning. The temperature was 21°F and he was visibly shivering. He'll likely be around till mid autumn depending on the weather.

Near the southern border of Winhall are numerous swamps and bogs. This time of year they're inviting places to wander with open sky, relatively clear water that runs swift from one swamp to another, dormant brush that you can actually see your way through, and with minimal threat of ticks as winter's chill lingers through early spring.

A spirited chorus of Wood frogs catches my attention while approaching a ghostly looking swamp. It's an antithetic sound coming from such a display of death and decay. "Ghost" swamps are relatively small areas with the corpses of trees felled into the water and left there. Though obvious a beaver did the felling, what's not obvious is why the trees were all felled around the same time, why so many of them were felled into the water, and why, after felling, didn't the beaver harvest the fresh branches for food instead of letting the trees lay, first to dry out, and then eventually to rot in the muck and stagnant water. This one is a fairly recent addition to the landscape in terms of years, but there are a few of these apparitional wetlands up here.

As always with Wood frogs, word spreads quickly that someone's approaching and things get hush in a hurry. Closer examination of the dark, still water reveals multiple egg masses.

Some time later while wandering north, an open, rocky place comes in to view, where for endless days and countless nights, through blazing heat, numbing cold, ferocious winds, pelting rain, and blizzard snows, British Soldiers have stood their ground... sort of.

Though British Soldiers may not ever have set eyes on this place, their namesake plant (not really a plant but lichen; a fantastic organism of algae and fungi) thrives here. My understanding is that the name refers to the bright red tops resembling the uniform of His Majesty's military during the American Revolution. To me they resemble deformed matches growing out of the ground conveniently located near rock for easy striking. Don't bother trying, I did as a kid, it doesn't work.

At The Pond

Mornings in the second trimester of spring often begin below freezing; remnants of winter chill quickly dispatched by the strong vernal sun... most days.

. . .

Cold air hovers above the water. Faint breezes bend rising wisps of mist. An orange sun peeks through the trees, brightening as it clears the horizon. Yellow-rumped and Palm warblers express their excitement as does a Ruby-crowned kinglet that shows its colorful headpiece before flitting away up into hemlock, spruce, fir, and pine. The forest is thick with the scent and accumulation of needles. As I walk with deliberate delay beneath the evergreens, the disorienting sensation of memory foam underfoot makes it difficult to balance. Thick, low lying branches with broken views of the pond obscure me from sight. A Northern flicker watches me from the exposure of its perch in the sun. I'm close, yet it hasn't moved. Minding my manners I look at it only briefly while pretending to scan a larger area it happens to be part of. Its markings of grey, brown, black and red on the head and neck are brilliant in the full sun.

Wind whispers through the pines as ravens call in the distance. There's a Bald eagle across the pond, where red swelling maple buds against a multihued backdrop of mixed evergreens provide the first hint of color among the dormant tree tops. A Song sparrow fugue spreads along the thicketed shore as recent arrivals stake their claims, while Swamp sparrows join the fray with their rattled rendition of junco speak. A tiny rear-wheel drive car with bias-ply tires screeches around a corner... Oh. Oops, it's a kingfisher darting over the water. Turning my head to catch a glimpse of it flying south, I notice patches of snow still on the mountain.

Wandering along and around the shoreline trying to reconcile the advantage of thick evergreen cover with the disadvantage how much noise I'm making, I stop to examine the Balsam fir growth. It's a wonderful display of species adaptation effecting different strategies to thrive within the same organism. Needle growth varies from flat to whorled depending on exposure of the branches and twigs along the length and depth of the tree... pretty smart for a piece of wood.

A lone Spring peeper sings from deep in the forest. Water lilies threaten to open in a sun-soaked, shallow cove. A beaver hovers in the water near its lodge in the shade. Wintergreen berries from last year persist. Chewing on a leaf I'm transported back in time and space; a squirt kid of eight years old with a mouthful of teaberry gum, exploring woods along the Mohawk River in Alplaus, NY.

Leaving the cover of snap-crackle woods for an exposed area of shoreline, I'm treated to a display of eagle aerobatics as a pair of mature Baldies dives and rolls, flying north over the water into a stiff, chilling wind. A lone male Common merganser feeds in white-capped water while three Mallards follow a goose bobbing in the wash.

The north wind bites through my clothes as I stand in the open, exposed to its full fury. It's one of those days (unlike most) when even the strong vernal sun is no match for the wind driven chill.

Holy Indifference of Life

Thick white fog hangs above a dormant, ice coated canopy. Broad spears of dark grey trunk pierce the frosted understory through an unrelenting mist. Endless dripping soaks unfrozen leaf litter while falling shards of ice bounce on the spongy forest floor. Stagnant light distorts my sense of time and space while I wander this unfamiliar world dinned with the constant clatter of dripping water and dropping ice. Birds and frogs stay hidden and silent in awe of the holy indifference of Life.

About five weeks after Vernal Equinox, this condition persisted for thirty-six hours. Wandering the woods during this time I neither saw nor heard a single passerine bird, or frog in or near any ponds.

Blending In

Within the forest, a society of animals understands and respects the rules that govern their rendition of civility. There are no wars in this society.

And while it's within these rules that govern to eat and be eaten, its citizens rely on scent, gestures, vocalizations, and displays to conduct their daily endeavors in acquiescent coexistence.

Woodland manners are foreign to most of us. We live in a different society. But if we have an interest in blending into the forest community instead of standing out like the pillaging primates we've come to be known as within the wood, perhaps we can study these manners. And who better to teach us than the creatures that live there?

It takes time and a certain degree of immersion that will test your mettle.

Enjoy.

Cascading Thoughts

Cool west winds keep black flies at bay as I navigate a steep northwest slope zigzagging my way toward the sound of water breaking on rock. A great chorus of migrating songbirds overlays the windswept canopy with notes unattainable by the finest symphony orchestras. Hermit and Wood thrushes, Scarlet tanagers, Rose-breasted grosbeaks, numerous warblers, vireos, and sparrows, along with a Winter wren fill the sound canvas to overflow inducing a cascade of thoughts...

"I would have gone straight up thirty years ago.
Is youth wasted on the youth?
Truth is black and white when you're young.
The shortest distance between two points is still a straight line.
This truth hasn't changed.
So what has?
Experience.
Is it part of evolution; an adaptation?
Can wisdom; learned, subjective, situational, be an adaptation?
Why not, if it furthers the evolution of a species?
Anyway, zigzagging is easier on my knees.
The Universe is kind to bestow wisdom on us as we decay.
Is decay the catalyst to broadened thinking?
What if it's your mind that's decaying?

How do you know?
Maybe I should stop."

I descend the north slope of the ravine through a small group of hemlocks to the top of the lowest chute. Three torrents run down its slightly stepped, nearly shear drop. The next step-up begins as one stream, splitting in two before reaching the lower cascade. The third chute up has a single torrent, filling a pool before plummeting toward the middle cascade. Above this, a steep, moss lined rivulet joins a stronger flow tumbling down into the ravine from the south side. Within the watercourse, rock slabs cling to the steep, while jagged boulders along and within tell of the ones that let go. Umbled white flowers of hobblebush and the greens and grays of moss and rock reflect in shiny pools of tannin tea, weak from a winter's brewing.

The Highlands III

About three thirds and a week more than one third of a season later...

       The earliest of the woodland spring flowers are blooming together in the Highlands. That's not to say there isn't some crossover in the other zones below, but only this high can you see Spring Beauties beginning so late together with Trout lilies, Painted and Red (should be burgundy) trillium, and of course, hobblebush. A few early ferns have been burned from the recent spate of cold, frost, and snow here. Tiny blue violets are also blooming where they can get enough sun through the still-dormant canopy. In open places the strawberries are in flower. Clintonia leaves are up as are wild oats (bellwort), Indian cucumber, and the Solomon's-Seals, though none are flowering yet. Even a few ginseng plants are visible. Certainly this is not an exhaustive list, but an example of some of the common plants of the forested Highlands. Deciduous trees are still dormant except for a tinge of green in select understory. Reindeer lichen is thick and healthy where it grows well up here. Looking closely, it seems an alien (yes, of the planetary variety), out of place among so many other "earthly" looking plants such as hobblebush; leggy limbed, broad green leaved, clear white flowered.

The month of May could be considered hobblebush month except for the fact that so many other causes have claimed May as their month, not the least of which is the EPA's American Wetlands month. I'll take this as a consolation since the highlands are also full of individual and connecting swamps, brooks, streams, and bogs. Not to hobble a dead horse, the USDA's Natural Resources Conservation Service webpage on hobblebush indicates that it's "a facultative upland non-hydrophyte that usually occurs in non-wetlands but may occur in wetlands." HUH? I'm pretty sure this means it can live in or out of the Highlands, and in or out of wetlands. At least that's been my experience with it. I'm just glad the humble hobble has received this much attention because after it blooms most people hardly know it exists except those of us that covet its fruit.

With the last weeks of leaf out about to happen in the Highlands, everything will begin accelerating as the calendar moves into June. There's a hint of the increasing momentum from high vantage points; the advance of green up the surrounding mountain slopes is thickest to about 1600', mixing with the grey/brown of dormant slopes through 2000' with only the Highlands left to be foliated. As a matter of fact 8 weeks of spring have brought little change to this area.

Bear In Mind

Wandering the northern Highlands in mid spring, bear sign is easier to find due to the still dormant trees, scant understory growth, and increased activity as they search for whatever limited food can be found at this time of year. Sows with new cubs in particular are busy making milk and that means eating a lot.

Walking an old skidder road adjacent to a series of small swamps, bear scat in varying degrees of decay are as numerous as Hansel's trail of pebbles. Some are months old and were buried in what little snow fell up here this past winter. Some are likely weeks old, others just days, and one aromatic deposit, still warm, lays only steps from a freshly torn apart punky birch log. I've missed the activity here by minutes. There's no need to describe the bouquet, it's as one might imagine. As for how I know it's still warm, there's something instinctive about being able to recognize fresh *Ursus poopus*. For one thing, it's fragrant. For another it may be an adaptation to let you know you shouldn't be in that place, or to get your spear ready if you have a craving for bear meat, though appetite isn't an instinct being triggered at the moment. But neither is flight.

I've never met a Black bear I didn't like, even the little "chevron" bear that was hanging around the house for a few days one late summer until it bluff charged me which triggered my own bluff charge resulting in its quick change of heart and direction. It was all quite harmless.

Drawn by the amount of beech wood I had recently cut and split, I understood the bears desire to investigate such an enormous olfactory bonanza to see if it yielded any beech nuts, but it continued to make stressed gestures in response to my presence escalating to the point of animated bluster. It was time to establish this area as my home. Maybe it was confused over ownership of the great aroma since I made no attempt to dissuade the investigative bear from indulging its nose, being more curious and eager to observe than alarmed by its presence. In the end a simple expression of "this is mine" on the part of the hominid was enough to establish the clear territorial boundary that the bear apparently needed as part of its understanding of me.

Giving the benefit of respect to whoever belongs to the steaming pile of *Poopus horribilus*, I wander off in the opposite direction of the swamps walking in a semi-open, shrubby area, with head down, hat brim blocking the sun. A recent Hollywood release comes to mind where an unfortunate fellow gets between a Grizzly sow and her cubs. She mauls him, he shoots her, she mauls him some more, he draws a knife, she comes at him again, they both roll downhill, and she lands on him. She's dead and he's an inch away from it. A bad day all around if ever there was one.

Rounding a thick brushy area I look up to see a beautiful bear not 50' in front of me. With the wind blowing in my direction, scent and sound are in my favor; it has no idea I'm here, and it's looking in the opposite direction. Looks like a mature male by the size of it. Turning its head in my direction it still seems to have no clue I'm here.

"Big Bear" uttered in a soft voice is enough to get its attention. Focusing its eyes on mine I can see the facial expression and body language change as if the whole thing is happening in slow motion. The poor bruin can't move fast enough away from me, crashing through the brush, disappearing into the woods. But uncharacteristic of such an event (I've had a few over the years) there's no continuous crashing through the woods, no snorts, no grumbles of discontent, nothing, only silence. I begin to notice the sound of scratching. It seems hurried. I fix my gaze in the direction of the sound waiting to see a big male bear scrambling skyward. But somehow I missed what had taken place in the time between seeing the bear initially, and watching it sprint for the cover of the forest.

Higher in the tree than I thought the sound was coming from; two small animals (more brown than black) are headed for the top of a large maple, stepping on each other along the way. It's a comical scene and in my entertained state I'm unable for a moment to piece together the story that I'm a part of. Cubs; comical, adorable, likely frightened, and mother; large, stressed, currently not visible but very close by and I, were all part of one of those moments I mentioned previously in Knock Wood.

Though the bear in mind only moments ago was a Grizzly who wasted no time in attacking what she perceived as a threat, this Black bear's response to me was to sprint for the woods in the direction of her young. If Black bears were of a different temperament, perhaps we too would have had a bad day as in the case of our motion picture counterparts. Nonetheless, this is a sow with cubs and as such deserves respect and consideration for the stress my presence has caused her. It may take a while before the cubs gain the courage (or suffer the hunger for mother's milk) before they come down. She certainly has my respect already, and gratitude as well for her non-aggressive response to my presence.

As I walk back in the direction I came, speaking in a loud enough voice to be understood as leaving, I ponder the nature of these gentle beasts. She is big enough to maul me, kill me, and have me for dinner, of that I'm sure. Yet the look in her mammalian eyes was familiar and unmistakable; worry. I had no idea at the time she was worried for her cubs, thinking it was a male, so the emotion I detected in her eyes was confusing and served to draw my attention away from the truth of the moment; the sight and sound of cubs scurrying up a tree escaped me.

It was another fascinating (and humbling) example of how our preconceptions can overrule a sufficient body of evidence available to our senses.

. . .

About five miles south and two thirds of a few weeks later...

As I wander the southern Highlands I once again come around a thicket (now very thick since leaf-out has occurred) to see a Black bear coming down the same path I'm going up, about the same distance away as the bear I saw most recently. I stop. Unaware of me it takes a few more steps in my direction before stopping, and then looks directly into my eyes. I prefer this from Black bears this close. It always seems the beginning of a dialog where each of us gives pause to allow the other to think before "speaking." He's a handsome brute with a large face, dark nose and tinges of brown toward his aft. My last encounter being of recent memory, I look and listen closely in the event I've misidentified another bear's gender and there are cubs around. The woods are quiet. There's no look of worry in this one's eyes and if I didn't think I was imagining it, I'd swear I could hear him breathing; slowly. Here we are; mammalian kin, distant cousins, different species, needing the same basic things to survive and thrive, yet each with limited knowledge concerning the customs of the other, sharing more or less a very tiny spec of forest.

I wonder what memories he's recalling at this moment and what impression he's getting of me as we stand, relaxed in body language, yet both obviously not yielding the trail to the other. He's big. The more I look at him the more I see the massiveness of his head, the thickness of his legs, and the overall girth of his body. And he's relaxed.

It's difficult to resist the urge to think we can get closer; perhaps even pet him, as he leans; head into my hip, and then be on our separate ways, sharing the bit of trail we're on while passing each other, instead of the reality that one of us has to give way. But this is the truth, and this is no bear to speak calmly to and back away from. There are no external stressors such as cubs, no physical barriers to his escape, no food cache to defend, no favorite female close by that he may think I have designs on, and finally, I'm alone.

With some reluctance not reflected in the tone of my voice I outright lie and tell him I'm bigger than he is. Without giving him time to laugh, I lie again, louder, raising my arms above my head. Looking a bit frazzled he turns and trots away up the path huffing and complaining. As I begin walking slowly, I keep a close eye on him. He stops after a few lumbering trots. I stop. As he looks back at me, I notice he turns his body at more of an angle toward me than away. I wonder about the flexibility of such a creature and if it's easier to turn his body a bit than to crank his neck around while positioned heading away from me. Again we stand there, wondering about each other. Again I run through the fantastical idea of him being ok with being petted...

As he turns his whole body directly toward me, my ancient hominid amygdala implores me to be more persuasive about who's going to yield this little bit of path so the other can pass. Raising my arms again as I begin walking with determination, I strongly insist, feigning

49

conviction that my ridiculous lie of being bigger than he is has merit and is absolutely true. After all, would I purposely walk in the direction of something I thought could harm me? He obliges my delusion and takes off running up the path again out of sight. Being appreciative of his yielding the path to me, I stop and wait a few moments before moving.

As I pass the area I last saw him, the bear isn't immediately visible, though he may still be quite close, watching and learning a bit more about *H. sapiens* behavior. In an effort to set a good example, I continue on at a relaxed pace without stopping or peering into the woods. If he's there, he's at a comfortable enough distance for him not to be crashing through the woods running away, and I feel as though stopping to look for him now (which, if he is watching will cause him undue stress) would be an insult to the good manners he showed by yielding the path to me.

Sometime later while sitting near a stream enjoying a pipeful of tobacco as part of my integrated woodland pest management, I compare my two most recent bear meetings which were quite different circumstances requiring different approaches.

↓ PLEASE READ CAREFULLY ↓

Black bears are free roaming, free living entities that do what they want when they want. And they're not small. I wasn't kidding when I said of the sow above that she could maul me, kill me, and have me for dinner. And in short order, the boar in my second story could do the same. Too many people forget this and end up causing trouble for themselves or the bears they encounter. And although I entertain the idea of a relationship such as a dog has with a

50

human, I know this *is not*, *should not*, and *will not* ever be a reality with bears (or any free roaming animal) I meet in my travels. Finally, (here's the disclaimer) writing about my experience outdoors does not express or imply any directions, instructions, or suggestions as to how *you* should approach your experiences, and anything you do that remotely resembles anything I've written about is an act of freewill on your part, and of no advisement of mine.

Having said that, I hope you have experiences with our mammalian kin that thrill you as much as my experiences with them have thrilled me.

A Conversation with Big Rock

"I don't mind being on this side of the road," Big Rock began. "It's nice being out of the hole I was in. I'd been there for so long it seemed natural; I used to think it was such a comfortable place. When I was left in that spot after the big ice went away I was content to watch the forest come closer and closer and finally grow up around me. I didn't realize I was being buried by the little leaves of those trees. I remember the day I saw human people for the first time. There were four of them, all wearing animal skins. They walked by swiftly without making a sound... and were gone. The next time I saw human people was a very long time after that. There were two of them with things that cut trees, and animals that I never saw before helping them to take the trees away and dig up the ground around me. I missed the forest and wasn't used to being in the sun anymore. Then, odd plants began to grow all around me and I was in the shade again. The human people would come and take things from those plants every year. But the plants were too close together and died every winter. I didn't like them. This went on for many years, and then suddenly stopped. The forest grew back slowly and I was happy once again to be surrounded by trees, though this new forest is different from the old. I would see human people walking in the forest from time to time. They came always with the intent of taking something. Sometimes it was the trees, other times animal people, and other times berries and nuts, plants and flowers. If there's something they want, they take it. They're always changing things, moving things, even the rocks. Always touching, moving, taking..."

"Excuse me," I said in a respectful tone, "but you're still looking at the world from that hole you were in."

Big Rock was silent.

"Everything that crawls, walks, flies, slithers and breathes takes from something else," I continued. "Some call it the circle of life. Living things live off other living things. There's constant movement from one form to another."

"So... I'm... not a living thing?" asked Big Rock in a disappointed voice.

We both sat in silence.

"I never thought of myself as not being alive," said Big Rock, breaking its silence again. "I always thought everything was alive. Isn't everything alive, even the clouds and rain and wind? What about snow and ice? Aren't they alive? They all move, don't they? The big ice that put me here... Wasn't that alive? It moved, well, very slowly... but it took pieces of me, and smoothed me out while it rolled over me, changing my form. Doesn't this make me part of your circle of life?"

"In a manner of speaking and in a way of seeing yes, everything is alive," I reply. "The Earth is a living planet with a liquid, moving core, with great continental plates shifting and colliding above it. There are mountain ranges and volcanoes above and below the oceans. There are still enormous sheets of ice like the one that put you here,

53

shaping and reshaping the landscape. There are winds, rain, snow, heat from the sun, lightening, rivers; all these things are part of the grand palette that life is painted on. But the definition of life as we know it is specific and some things, though living in the broader sense as components of the Earth, do not fit this definition."

Big Rock is silent.

Night falls.

Morning comes.

Big Rock says nothing.

Days pass and I now realize I've lost a connection few people ever make.

Genuine sadness wells up in me as I decide to leave Big Rock alone again in the forest for endless ages. Even if it's still self aware, Big Rock is no longer willing or able to communicate. As I walk away a great crack resounds through the forest from behind me. I can't look. I've broken its heart.

Waking to the rumbling remnant of a thunder clap I hold my breath and quiver. "It was a dream," I think to myself... "A dream." Getting up from my nap at the edge of a small pond not far from Big Rock, I navigate through the thickening woods to find that old familiar log road, despite the pouring rain. Turning west I continue on and see Big Rock from a distance. With a smile of relief, I quicken my pace, but when I arrive my heart sinks. Big rock is split in half.

At The Pond II

About three thirds of a few weeks later...

Approaching the pond it's evident that things are advancing here ahead of the Highlands by a week or more. Looking at the forest as a whole from the understory through the canopy, light green is beginning to fill in spaces between trees... and the bugs are out. A dense cloud of black fly admirers is so enamored with me that they even stop to wait when I take pause in my walking. Within the confines of thick evergreens, the hum of their wings is louder than the soft breezes blowing through the forest. Occasional morning gusts disperse the cloud.

In addition to the birds present the last time I was here, today there are ovenbirds, a Winter wren, Wood thrushes, White-throated sparrows, redstarts, juncos, Purple and Gold finches, Black-throated Green and Chestnut-sided warblers, a catbird, kingbirds, chickadees, Blue jays, and a pair of Tree swallows.

It appears as if the same two eagles are still here. One perches above a Wood duck box for twenty minutes before flying off to the south and "tagging" its partner, which I haven't seen until now, perched in a tree across the pond. It takes flight in my direction.

Watching a large bird of prey through binoculars conveys the holy, unmitigated freedom of their existence: Seer eyes scan the horizon upon their lofty thrones of wind as unchallenged wings command the air around them. Is there any grander life than life on the wing?

Back on earth, American toads perform, "We're really Ultra-Endurance Crickets," the shadblows have already shed their flowers, little water beetles scurry about in semi-circles outrunning, then colliding with one another, the Common merganser has a mate, and a female Mallard with five ducklings paddle away from shore as I approach. I chuckle at the sight of such little things moving so fast in the water.

The Highlands IV

About half a third season later...

A cool, breezy blue sky, millions of new leaves undamaged by a summer of insect browsing, a Broad-winged hawk's piercing whistle, an ovenbird's relentless search for its lost teacher, and a slow moving army of Red efts are the first impressions of the day.

Streams that roared toward the Winhall River weeks ago, now gurgle their sinewy courses through the woods. A phoebe hunts along one such stream, perched in the shadows, flitting out into the sunlight to snatch a snack.

As I cross an open area where the grasses are still short, small white flowers of strawberry catch my eye reflecting the sun from their fully exposed locations, and ant hills everywhere, dominate the Lilliput landscape. Less numerous, but more curious are the small shallow holes of recent digging; round, in soft dirt without clear claw, paw, or hoof print left behind as clues to who made them.

Re-entering the woods I continue south and notice movement in a small patch of sunlight far ahead. Through binoculars I see a lone doe acting jittery. I wonder what she sees, smells, or hears. Studying her hyper-awareness I ponder those questions and why she's alone. It's difficult to judge her size, but maybe she's about to give birth, or has already; maybe she's lost a fawn. Rather than embrace my conjecture I accept it as inconclusive. Waiting till she's out of sight, her direction of travel in mind, I wander away not wanting to add to whatever stress she's experiencing.

Further along, now in the Lye Brook Wilderness, another of the "ghostly" looking swamps comes in to view. The thick tangled screen of leafless, light-grey limbs creates a disorienting illusion of smoke. As I approach, proximity exposes illusion and each limb, branch, and twig now visible, reflects in the still black water. A pair of Green frogs review escape plans with increasing urgency in what sounds like a vehement disagreement as to what to do about the interloper. Two plops into liquid obsidian tell me an agreement's been reached as I approach.

Exploring where the tributaries of the Winhall River percolate, seep, and pond before gaining momentum by losing elevation I can't help but wonder what it was like here a thousand years ago. It's a shame, criminal even, that the oral history of this place is gone. Surely someone knew of this area in the thousands of years it was habitable before European contact. My understanding is that trade routes between the Connecticut River Valley and the Lake Champlain basin crossed over the spine of the Green Mountains along the rivers flowing down its east and west slopes. Are we to believe that people traveled along the West River but didn't notice the Winhall with easy access from where it flows into the West? Less than six and a half miles in lies a beautiful flat area of over 150 acres with "river frontage," suitable as a protected summer encampment for a growing family band. It wouldn't take much from this area to hunt up into the surrounding highlands using the river and its tributaries as main sources of navigation. I sit against a tree pondering this line of reasoning, close-eyed, open-eared.

The ponds are bigger than I remember, not the swamp-thicket linked habitats I'm familiar with. The heavy scent of balsam, spruce, hemlock and pine; pungent-sweet decongestant, hangs thick, compressing the air at ground level. Secrets of a time long forgotten whisper through the needled canopy of mast-size pine. I'm out of place, but at peace. Following a narrow, beaten path through the forest I see open water ahead, hear voices, and catch a whiff of wood smoke. The path continues in the direction of the voices. Not sure what to do I wait and listen. Too far away to hear their words I begin walking, slow and deliberate down the path. The smoke is visible now and the voices louder, yet words aren't reaching my ears, just tones and inflections. There are children. Men are laughing. The soft spoken melody of multiple women conversing, closer than the other voices, still yields no discernible words. Footsteps approach me on the path. I hide behind a great pine tree much wider than the width of my body. Thunder rolls over the landscape approaching with speed. It's unusual for a storm to move so fast.

I wake to the rumbling of a jet high overhead, its sound bending and bouncing along the landscape, muffled and amplified by shifting winds. "Some thunderstorm," I think to myself as I move my legs and flush a turkey that had wandered within feet of me while I was asleep. Both of us, frightened by the other find our feet in an instant; the turkey transferring locomotion to its wings, and I, also flapping my wings, brush off the forest duff and begin walking again.

Savoring the smell of Balsam fir while walking through a grove of little ones two to four feet high heating up in the sunlight, I reach for a pinch of fresh needles. Both these and the spruces are pushing out new shoots with the firs slightly ahead. I prefer the taste of Balsam to that of the spruces but this nip of needles seems a bit sharp. Spitting them out, I find a tighter cluster, lower down and shaded. "Mmm... better."

Still somewhat in the fog of a nap unfinished, I notice moose prints, finally, after all these weeks of wandering in good habitat. I follow the tracks through some open hardwoods, then across a soggy tussock field to the edge of a sun baked bramble thicket; ticky-weed heaven. Given my pay grade for the day I decide to go back over the tussocks and around the thicket rather than through.

"Why doesn't this look familiar," I think to myself when I re-enter the woods; a tall spruce/fir grove. "Did I come this way?"

The wind blows, trees sway. Familiar sounds catch my attention; whining, creaking, moaning, and haunting meows like those of kittens. I remember the last time I heard that meow sound I was...

"Great."

Getting lost isn't a problem; that's easy. Even finding your way back isn't the hardest part. The worst part of it all is that it supplants your confidence in the one person you thought you could count on: You. Some days are worse than others. Last time wasn't terrible. Today sucks. I'm completely disoriented. I may as well be in Siberia. Good time to sit, pack a bowl full of tobacco, and have a smoke.

Deer flies dominate the airspace around me, pipe smoke keeps them moving. As I pull out my map and compass, cognitive behavior is no longer a struggle and a sense of decorum returns as the rush of chemicals that urged me to escape through the forest by running, relent. It seems an evolutionary conundrum that we should continue to have this reflex when we have such an ability to reason...

"Yep, I'm feeling better," blurts out of my mouth.

Now correctly oriented with an approximate present location, armed with my Savineli Roma securely clenched between my teeth, I stand up and wander west toward a route that will take me home.

Water

It takes two atoms of Hydrogen and one atom of Oxygen to make water. That's it; three atoms, one molecule: POOF! Water.

Well, not quite POOF! My understanding is that Hydrogen appeared less than a second after the Big Bang but had to wait around while gravity collected and compressed it enough to ignite it; forming stars. Then gravity further compressed these stars, sufficient to raise their core temperatures to manufacture Oxygen (among other things). T-H-E-N... those stars spread these elements through the cosmos via solar winds or exploding. After that, the Hydrogen and Oxygen had to meet up while planets were forming around *other* stars and then bond under the right temperature and pressure to make... POOF! Water.

It's a little more complicated than this, but my point, without causing a black hole in the attention span of the reader, is that water is a fantastic wonder of space.

. . .

Sitting on a boulder in the shade of overhanging trees, where the Winhall River and one of its tributaries meet, water seems much less fantastic. Here, among the thick, mid-June forest where every living thing depends on it for life, it's tangible. I feel it; spraying on my skin, hear it; coming and going, see it; flowing toward and away, smell it;

liquid splashing and vapor rising from sun-warmed rock. Although more than noteworthy and quite consequential, *how* water came to be means little to us. We're not drawn to molecular water. We're drawn to water that springs from the ground, flows into rivers, runs into oceans; water that supports life within and without.

As a kid I remember hearing that we came from monkeys. That made sense to me. But hearing that monkeys came from fish? Well, that was difficult to imagine. As an adult I'm fascinated by the idea that the reason we're so smitten with water is because that is where we came from. But who knows, maybe we're space aliens. For now, I'll go with the fish story (no pun intended).

The waters seem to speak, one to another as they run, splash and gurgle by. It's a soothing sound compared to the noise in my head about monkeys, fish, and space aliens. Splaying myself out on the boulder, I take a deep breath, close my eyes, and ponder the importance of water and the idea of being a fish.

River and Stream each believed they were more important than the other and asked Loon who was greater. River argued that it was longer, deeper, and wider than Stream, but Stream argued that River would be nothing more than a trail of mud without Stream to feed it.

Loon, wisest and oldest of all birds, knew River to rise in anger, and considered the outcome of its answer.

"River," said Loon. "Without you there would be no guiding waterways and no brackish zones along the seacoasts for the immeasurable number of my relatives that

travel from north to south and back again each year." Loon continued, "But many others also live beyond your shores in the deep forests and high mountains where Stream lives. And as you know, I prefer the solitude of small coves on lakes. Most of these and many swamps and ponds are fed by Stream."

"But I need to know who is greater," said River.

Loon thought some more. Then, looking up at Sun, spoke again, "Sun is greater. Without Sun there would be no plants, no animals, no life, only darkness. And if Sun decided to swell as you often do when you're angry, everything within you would dry up and die. Yes, Sun is greater."

Stream, hearing only what it wanted to hear without listening closely to Loon, began splashing and gurgling at the idea that Loon thought it was greater than River.

With its deep red eyes staring at Stream, "You are greater than Sun?" Loon asked.

"Greater than Sun? No, no but I'm greater than River because Life put trees along my banks and they shade my water. This way, even if Sun did swell in anger, I'd never dry out. I think Life knew I was greater and so put the trees there to protect me from Sun!"

Shaking his head, Loon tried again, "If Sun swelled enough to dry River's water, then the trees along your banks would die and the ground water that springs up to feed you would dry..."

At that moment, Life spoke. "You two waters support and carry life through the mountains, forests, valleys, and lowlands, and then join with your Elder; the Ocean. None of you, not even your Elder is greater than another..."

Loon sees me watching and torpedoes toward me.

I try swimming away but can't move.

My back bends to the breaking point as Loon catches me it its bill.

Jolting awake with debilitating back pain, I pay in full the price of falling asleep on cold stone. As I roll over and stare into the water, a small Brook trout looks at me with disgust. Its ancestors risked everything to crawl out of the water so I would one day have a flexible spine and neck. Now look at me.

This Might Not Go Well

With heightened senses from a night in the forest, my eyes still closed, I hear them walking. First it's turkeys descending from the ridgeline above, then a lone hominid in typically hurried, bipedal fashion; a huntsman enters the woods below. He calls. Turkeys express apprehension, clucking softly to one another, giving away their position. The hunter calls again, inciting a Barred owl response. Turkeys gobble. The pattern repeats itself as hunter and quarry advance on my position. This might not go well.

A godzurkey screamgobble splits the air, bombastic caterwauling fills it. Robins launch a vehement peeping offensive against the owls. Blue jays arrive; shrieking. The caterwauling ends. Alarm calls continue, one owl ignores the passerine posse, the other flies away. Jays give chase. Unrelenting robins force the remaining owl from its perch. Through all this commotion, the calling stops while thrushes, vireos, and warblers frame the unfolding drama in a chorus of normalized tranquility. After the owls leave, peace is restored.

Calling resumes. One turkey responds; imitating the hunter, another gobbles; interrupting the songbirds. With softer calls spaced farther apart, the hunter adjusts technique. No replies. Another attempt... Yellow-bellied sapsuckers reply with vocalizations similar to a turkey's non-gobbling gibberish.

The huntsman leaves with no quarry.

I wonder about the behaviors of these and the other birds this morning: Robins and Blue jays were so aggressive toward the owls, yet now they conceal their presence with silence. Robins fly from several directions always back to the same tree, the same limb. Blue jays busy themselves in similar fashion. It's a good indication that young are in the nests.

Beech and maple limbs wave slowly on soft breezes while fresh, unfurled leaves remain still. A Winter wren arrives to scold me for being here, and then flits back into thick forest cover as the sun clears the ridgeline above.

The black flies are early today. It's time to move.

What's All the Raven About

With one third of the third third of spring left on the calendar, the woods are in full leaf-out after recent cool, rainy weather. A late night shower followed by a gentle cold front gives this morning a crisp, washed-lettuce fragrance.

Shrieking Blue jays spear the silence above a damp forest. A juvenile raven implicates the jays in a harassment complaint; a call for help hidden in witch-scream: "MOM! MOM!" Another raven, lacking the emotion of the first, lodges a second complaint in a softer witchy-scream: "Mom Mom." The two jays continue their binary blitzkrieg as the ravens summon aid; "MOM! Mom..." A third jay utters metallic gurgle amidst the shrieking. The cacophony quiets.

A Hermit thrush breaks the silence wondering what's all the raven about. A sudden, bellowing raven "GWONK!" echoes through the forest re-igniting the incendiary squabble. If blindfolded I'd guess dinosaurs, not birds, were above me in the canopy while the Hermit's fluty inquiry adds to the surrealness of the scene. As though pausing to hear the thrush, the passerine combatants cease fire again.

"MOM?" interrupts the Hermit's song, more questioning than demanding. A single Blue jay shriek follows. A long drawn out "M-O-M?" spreads out over the canopy. I fight the temptation to bad manners of imitating while the two juvenile ravens scream, "MOM! Mom, MOM! Mom."

Frenzied shrieking and furious witch-scream engulf the forest as two adult ravens arrive. The raucous is deafening. My head spins in aural confusion as sounds jump from witch-scream to the Jurassic period and on to the Oligocene epoch as yowls of chimpanzees replace screams of dinosaurs... Or so it sounds.

Straining Blue jay voices draw clan members from the surrounding forest stepping up their offensive; darting in and out of close proximity to the ravens, frustrating the adults with speed and agility. The juveniles continue screaming, "MOM! Mom. An adult guards its position growling and snarling. It threatens counter attack. But the jays know they have the advantage in the confines of the tight canopy.

Retreat begins with one adult raven flung high above tree-top on whooping wings and witchy screams. Blue jays swarm like mad hornets in pursuit. Silent and stealthy, the second adult drops into the forest weaving 'round tree trunk and limb. Accelerating to gain position on the jays, it bursts through the canopy scattering the blue-feathered swarm.

As the two adult ravens circle back, the re-grouped jays descend on the juveniles again.

Frantic wing beats and cries of "Mom" push through the blue cloud of jays as they ignore the airborne juvenile and focus on the stubborn one; witch-screaming, frozen to its perch. Patient parents circle nearby while even the Blue jays grow tired of the incessant cries and break off, flying away.

Croaking locator calls and squawks of encouragement fade as the three airborne ravens travel north over the ridgeline into the valley below without waiting for the stubborn one to follow.

After forty minutes I leave the screaming raven and head for home. I've seen this happen a number of times before. The juveniles give in after a while and head in the direction of the rest of the family, but this one is particularly stubborn. As I wander out of the woods I wonder why.

Last Night

A silver-white disk floats on lavender clouds above the steel-grey horizon. In the dimming of day a Hermit thrush's elegant epitaph bids farewell to the light, while blue sky backdrop varies in hue across the advancing dome of night.

Leaving the comfort of its lavender pillow, brightening with each degree of rise, the full moon casts a chalky glow across the landscape. I make the mistake of looking directly at the now hot-white light, cancelling my night vision. With eyes closed, I focus on other senses.

Forest duff exhaling in the cool night air seeps out along the wood's edge, bramble flower and grass scent stick to the moistening ground. Mosquitoes hover close, testing and probing my barrier of repellent as bats flutter near enough to feel their wing thrusts. Coyotes bark and yip in the distance. Many footsteps traverse the forest, some slow and deliberate, others trotting by lithe and swift. Grey tree frogs converse over a nearby seep, asking questions without answers, while bullfrogs bellow from an undisclosed location.

Phosphor-green flash of lightening bugs seize my attention as I open my eyes again. Dozens flash close by in the tall grasses and brambles of the clearing. Dozens more blink inside the wood's edge making it difficult to tell which are the bugs' and which are the blinking eyes of shadow creatures peering out from the forest. They're hiding in the shadows. But I see them. They're real. At peace with them and myself, bug net over my head, slunk down in my sleeping bag, I close my eyes again and listen to the last night of spring.

. . .

I wake to the fanciful yammer of blaring caterwaul as Barred owls gather 'round the clearing in the wee hours of the morning. Elongated moon shadows twinkle with phosphorescent green, eclipsing the stars. Moist, still air, hangs heavy with the scent of ground and leaves. Despite the yammer of gathering owls, I struggle to stay awake. Incomprehensible peace of the moment pulls me under as I float off, adrift in a world somewhere between dreaming and waking.

Last Morning

First break of dawn brings an end to the revelry of Lightening bugdom. Few remain; weak, tired stragglers from a long night of unsuccessful courtship. There's an unusual absence of bird song until a Hermit thrush; inimitable wielder of woodwind, peels back the dark induced silence. A steady breeze; more the sound of whooshing water in a small stream than wind through leaves, cools my exposed skin. A robin bursts into song joining its cousin for morning vespers, while a Wood thrush, deep in the forest adds to the congregation of they who summon the sun. Across the clearing, reflected light of the growing dawn dapples the shadowy wall of trees, their tops a jagged horizon without individual form.

The heavy dew is a slight discomfort... lying on the ground in a sleeping bag, half hominid, half grub, everything's soaked. But what a unique night it was. Astronomical twilight occurred at 23:00 and again around 03:00 this morning, leaving only five hours of total darkness. But with moonrise at 20:30 and moonset at 05:30, these last two days of spring never saw the dark of night.

As soft lavender clouds against a pale blue sky turn salmon pink, slow deliberate hoof steps give away three deer while they browse beyond the clearing, confident within the woods edge. I see a leg... then an ear over there... then another leg... body... head... and tail as they dissolve into the woods. A small downdraft grabs the long slender branches of a woods edge beech, pulling and releasing them in an instant; a rush of wind and dancing limb. A nearby nest of White-faced hornets wakens. A short sharp gust, like a spot shower before a downpour, drops onto the clearing without hitting the trees. Salmon clouds fade to pale white below, while darkening to heather above.

Peeping and squealing and the furious flapping of robin's wings explode from the far end of the clearing. From the ground I can't see what's happening, but it sounds urgent and dire. An ovenbird joins the commotion with its own rendition of robin sized peeps and squeals when emerging from the woods edge, a Red fox, bird in mouth, trots toward me proud as a peacock. So enamored with itself and its latest achievement it appears oblivious to my presence; lying on the ground, propped up on an elbow. As it approaches looking down the sloped clearing I can see a juvenile robin in its mouth. To my absolute delight and surprise, the fox stops a few feet from me, finally getting a sense or whiff of something amiss while it stands still, assessing. In the faintest of voices I whisper, "Good morning." With the reaction of a cat, it pops straight up in the air without an apparent means of locomotion and turns 180° before reclaiming ground which it hits running with an effortless stride of elongated limbs; a glorious display of grace and beauty disappearing back into the woods through the gauntlet of frantic robins while still holding on to breakfast. Through the woods behind me to the west, I hear the fox trotting south again, now safe from giant hominoid grubs lying about.

The robins mourn their lost one in silence while other birds join the congregation. Common yellowthroats, Eastern wood pewees, Least flycatchers, Eastern phoebes, Red-eyed vireos, Downy woodpeckers, ovenbirds, Yellow-bellied sapsuckers, Scarlet tanagers, Black-capped chickadees, White and Red-breasted nuthatches, Tufted titmice, Song sparrows, Dark-eyed juncos, White-throated sparrows, Black-throated Green warblers, a Summer warbler, a Winter wren, Pileated woodpeckers, and Hairy woodpeckers all contribute to the collection plate of honors given the sun on this last morning of spring.

Across the cerulean veil that hides the heavens, clear light of the rising sun refracts through wisps of cloud casting a golden glow to the moment. I shake off the dew, pack up my things and leave.

Last Breath

My eyes struggle to find any sign of trail in undisturbed leaves through the dense, lush woods, while the sun; flaming, yellow in the west, illuminates my way. Familiar landmarks cannot guide me; the view in all directions is cloaked in a curtain of green. I continue walking, reading compass and elevation and noting the shadows that dance above me. For as many times as I've done this, you'd think I could keep my focus on where I'm going. But I can't, ever. Resisting the urge to turn back I arrive at my destination with little time to spare before Summer Solstice.

Thirteen weeks ago I watched my last winter lit fire fade at this old fire pit. It felt almost sacrilegious to defile the holy moonlit darkness with man-made fire that night, but nothing could dishonor and perhaps anger the sun more than to light a ritual fire during the day. I refrain, with or without approval of my ancestors.

Warm and inviting in these last moments of spring, here among mature hardwoods with profuse understory, every inch of ground exposed to light is populated with woodland plants, grasses, and ferns. Above and within the canopy soft breezes flow down from the ridgeline behind. Though warm, humidity is low making it pleasant to be out. I chuckle thinking about my hypothermic state thirteen weeks ago. 12°F is a long way from the 87°F reached earlier today.

Above and below me in a cascade of ledges, deep green moss clings to moist, shaded rock and feathery ferns grasp pockets of forest duff wedged between cracks; a delicate Lilliput world where one step scars as much as any careless logging in the forest. These ledges tell of time long ago when ice covered them and filled the basin below, when melt water carved cascades and falls, when bare rock was the landscape for millennium, waiting for tree line to advance.

Serpentine sound waves lilt down the hillside as a veery spins its spiral song. The fluty warbles of a Wood thrush percolate within the concealing canopy. Soft breezes exchange ideas and decide on new directions, while a few trees click and squeak in opposition to the changes. Other than this the woods are quiet, its residents still napping from the heat of the day.

Spring takes its last breath in the form of a Broad-winged hawk's piercing call, and at 18:24 summer arrives with a coaxing gust as shaded air cools and slumps down this east facing slope.

On cornflake leaves through tangled wood, up over ridges and down onto flats, I travel in a wide arc to exit the forest. Walking with deliberation, the last few months whiz by. A moth flies past my nose. I remember last winter night and first spring day, the birds, the animals, miles logged, the naps and dreams, the river, the bears, the Highlands and ponds, getting lost twice and...

What's this swamp doing here?

Wait...

Where am I?

Great.

www.ingramcontent.com/pod-product-compliance
Lightning Source LLC
Chambersburg PA
CBHW032153020426
42334CB00016B/1267